i'm sorry, i fell

but your memories tinted rain drops caught me
instead

Nayasha Jena

for all those who are here to read the *'falling in love'*
kind of stuff.

I'm sorry, this book only contains instances of me
falling into a *gutter.*

author's note

Hello, lovely people. I'm Nayasha- which is pretty clear from the cover page. Well, I'm almost seventeen or might be even seventeen when I publish this. I'm completely clueless about what to write and how to write an author's note. Is it where you describe what a person would find in the book? If that's the case then, It's all *him* and my love for him. All his little belongings and how they turn into the words that fill the void inside my head. All the texts that I type but then hit backspace faster than my brain could comprehend. All the rejections I wear when he talks about *her*.

There's so much to write about him that I can't even decide which one to write about. The unaware pain he causes or the burning ointment he applies right after that. He is so full of words that leaves me speechless. He is so full of emotions that leaves me numb. He wants a best friend who would laugh at his silly talks and not a girl who'd fall in love with them. I could go on and on about how I can't not stop writing about him.

But at some point in time, I realise it is not him I write about. Those are all the lovely ideas I create about him. Maybe, he is not what I picture him to be. Maybe, he is not the one I'd stay in love with. It's all *maybes* and *what-ifs* that I'm afraid of. But nevertheless, he makes me feel things on a different spiritual level which I think is advantageous because I can write poems about them, right? You see, it's all about loving him so much silently but in retrospect if one day I stop loving him it would start feeling like a whole part of my life was merely a lie. So I write, if not in the real world, maybe he could be mine in my made-up universe.

Talking about my poems, initially, they weren't about love, though. I had phases of nature poetry, and dark poems and then somehow slipped into the romance genre. The first book I wrote- yes, this is my second book. The first book is called *"Polychromatic Musings"* and is available on Amazon and Flipkart *(but I'd strongly suggest not reading it. God, I sucked at literature back then. I mean, I still am not thaaaat good but okay-ish, I guess.)* So, where was I? Oh yes, that book showcases my entire journey of what I was and what I am now, I mean sort of. Fourteen-year-old me was too moved by the idea of having this ability of writing. I mean, it's okay. This is a process. What if I hadn't started writing at all? *(Thanks to my best friend. She's a lovely girl.)*

Blank pages are intimidating to me. Writing the first line is so frustrating. It's almost as frustrating as choosing between two of my favourite singers *(I might die for the guy I like but I live for these people.)* I usually go through a lot of writer's block and I can't really figure out why. Probably because- *blacks out* Well, that calls for another writer's block. I'm sorry, I don't know what I am even writing. As I said, I am not a professional writer, so that's all I had to say.

Or maybe, I can pretend I am aware of these things and say something that'd be more useful to you. Like- do what you love and love what you do *(maybe?)*. If life gets hectic, take a break, lay back, forget everything you have to complete, all the assignments, homework, and client meetings and take a deep breath. It is not the end. *(I don't care if you've heard this a million times before. A million and one times wouldn't cause any harm.)* Failing at one aspect of life opens a door of success to another. *(That's what my mamma says.)* The more you keep yourself engaged, the happier it keeps you. Try new things and experiment with your life cause you only live once. *(An absolute original statement. Yes.)*

And for those who desperately want to love and be loved,
someone wise once said-

"Love happens to you, you don't happen to love."
(Phew. Good job, Nayasha.)

✦ ✦ ✦

acknowledgement

I would still have been nothing without some people in my life and now, I'm writing an entire book. All because of them. These mere pieces of pages filled with *'thank yous'* don't even compare to the amount of love, respect and gratefulness I have for them.

Starting with the person who always waited for the jingle sound of the iron shoe rack whenever he was told that I was going to visit him. I owe so much to you, *Aja*. I miss you and I hope you're bestowing your love on me from wherever you are.

A basket full of *'thank yous'* to *Aai, Maa, Bapa, Silu Dada, Bada Maa, Bada Bapa, Gedu Bapa* and *Bini Maa* for believing in me and considering me capable of carrying all their expectations.

Lots of kisses to all my *Mausis* for babysitting me and spoiling me *(and I appreciate that)*.

Bubu Mamu, I aspire to be as funny and charismatic as you are. Just letting you know guys, I don't have to wait for Christmas every year. I just need to drive some 200 km to meet my Santa. Thank you and I love you so much.

Thank you, *Mami Apa* and *Piisa*. You've been very motivating. Now I know, *Mami Apa*, there's absolutely no age for playing candy crush.

All the packets of pens you've stolen from me, *Sibun Bhai*, good for nothing though you are, I sincerely hate to admit that I love you.

Kunu Apa, oh my god. How am I supposed to thank you for everything you are to me? Next time you visit me, I'm not leaving you again. *(Also lots of kisses for lending me your Netflix account.)* And hugs for the rest of my family who treats me like I'm the biggest star *(but I'm only 5'1, by the way.)*

Disha (d.s), bestie, you can stop canoodling now. You know what you mean to me *(literally, nothing.)* You were the reason I started writing in the first place. Girlie goes on inspiring people with her crazy sweet tooth and a broken heart. Nevertheless, I should thank you for everything you've been in my life, most of all, for the joker I've always needed. Moreover, even if you have this entire book in your WhatsApp chat, it's an order for you to buy it.

Thank you *Priyaranjan* for being the mom I never wanted and giving me reality checks every time I got carried away with the thought of my ideal life. *"How could you burn an omelette?!"* is what I get reminded of when I hear your name. I promise I gave up on cooking a long time ago but I also hope one day I'll meet a worse chef than you, haha. *(This is what you get for not letting me eat your food but I love you.)*

Yash and *Preeti*, you guys have been a complete pain in the ass but somehow, you still have my heart. I have been living my teenage life vicariously through you people. I have seen the world through your eyes and this much credit, I guess, would be enough to convince you that y'all definitely need to gift me packs of chocolates.

Seshan, I am so glad we met. You don't even realise how grateful I am because you are the reason for half (no maybe, a quarter) the things I am today. Thank you so much for every little inconvenience you've caused in my life that has helped me recognise my true self. And the sweetest part is that you've never stopped supporting me.

Warmest hugs to *Swayam* (topper, hmmph.), *Alisha* (comfort person), *Akanshya* (always the rowdy one), *Pallavini* (try making sense the next time you speak, please but ilysm), *Saswati* (nothing's stopping us from rating guys), *Subham* (ilysm, Chinara, for being the bigger person amongst the two of us), *Priyankas* (one's a lesson; thanks for a poetry inspiration and the other's an angel, muah), *Ronit* (I felt obliged to put you in here.

Just kidding, ily), *Subhakant* (my insane other half), and all my friends who have never backed out from supporting me.

I would have been still failing English and Maths if I didn't have *Lisa Ma'am* and *Sir* with me. My second parents, thank you so much for being in my life. My love and respect for you can't be put into words.

Mamma and *Papa*, I might have this little ability to put my thoughts into paper, yet I am short of words right now. Thank you so much for moulding me into the amateur poet I am today. Anything I say, wouldn't be enough to repay you for everything you've done for me. *Bhai*, you're the loveliest. Though you can't understand a single word of this, being a sister of a child with autism has honestly been the bigger hand behind me being the most sensitive person I've ever known. I love you the most.

Finally, a huge thank you to all my readers and all others for supporting me. Thank you for picking up this book and deciding to go through the mess that I have tried to arrange in these bundled pages. And I hope it makes sense. Truly, I can never stop loving you, people.

Yours lovingly
Nayasha <3

✦ ✦ ✦

i'm

sorry

oasis

maybe she was the mistake
and I was the regret.
somehow, **you looked at me
for all she was.**

(*and she got the beautiful part
I got the ugly love, instead.*)

Up till 3 AM,
darkroom, escape room
I played with myself.
going through our conversation,
starting from that day
you sent me a write-up.
a cold breeze gushed
into my ribs,
a huge wave of love, anxiety,
guilt, hatred and angst
engulfed my entire headspace.

//where the hell did we go wrong?//

my eyes lingered on those
pretty *(sympathetic)* words

when you said you'd be there for me.
anytime.

(to mend me, I assumed
but you mend and left me broken
again, instead).

I wonder who's at fault.
I wonder if this is all stupid.
I wonder if you really ever cared.

what were you? a magic?
or just an illusion?
sometimes, you were the
the monster under my bed,
(haunting me every time but my
only company when I thought
I was drowning).

and sometimes you were just
the worst temporary fix in my
best fantasies
(while my grave had already
settled itself beside
our wrecked Titanic).

~nayasha

complications

I don't think I should love you.

(but I do. God, stop me, please)

hoping you'd think I'm not stupid
I've now read all your self-help books
while my favourite romance
novels gather dust on my shelf,

like my poetry.
like all my feelings for everyone else.
like all the other people around me.

every time, I fall, I fall harder
claiming that I can't love anyone
more than that.

can I love someone more than I love you?
can I love someone as I love you?

I hope I do...and I hope I don't.

what's better than this love?
what's worse than this heartbreak?

a daily unintentional heartbreak
put up on my timetable,
under every period.

you live, you break me.
you breathe, you break me.
your words, they break me.
your silence, it breaks me.

I wish I had never heard your voice.
I wish to regret letting your
guitar strings scratch my heart.

every time you talk,
you always change the direction
of our *'i-don't-know-wherever*
-it's-heading' relationship,

upon asking for a dream superpower,
I swear, it'd be infiltrating your mind,
I'm not anxious about why
you aren't talking to me.
I am anxious thinking about-

'do I even cross his mind?'

you didn't enter my life with notice
but I guess these days are the
notice period of you leaving.

*(my love cost my patience, my peace
and my poems)*

I shouldn't love you, now, should I?
*(only if unloving you was as easy as
asking this question)*

I shouldn't text you, should I?
I should let you go, shouldn't I?
but just one word from your side,
and I know I'll be betraying myself.

*//Guess, I've got a thing
for complicated guys.//*

~nayasha

the flawed hairdo

an unreasonable headache
the pretty floral scrunchie
swirling pink and yellow on
black
my hair held tightly by it.
the hair bears it all day,
bears it till it's past bedtime.
it slides down,
a slow, hurtful ride
like your embrace, **once,**
slid down my skin.
a peaceful pain lingers
in my scalp,
burning cold air
gushing into the holes
on my body that once
fitted your darts.
it slides down
with **a few strands of**
lost romance
tangled around it.

but it's too *beautiful*
to throw away
(too *strong* to just
simply forget)

*//so, I tie my pain with your failed
love every single day.//*

~nayasha

autumn's the only season I know

you're here, right next to me. gripping my waist,
with that very hand of friendship and god, that smile of
yours
I fell harder than I should have.

perfect, isn't it? (of course.)

until I realise, I'm not the reason for it. (anymore? I
never was)
the photographer still clicks pictures of the two of us,
you look at me with those lovely eyes.

an unintentional faking of love.

truth sealed my lips and philosophies of the 'present' tell
me to
love you when I can.

time is slipping through my fingertips
autumn air whispers that maybe, I am not the one.
my embarrassment snaps back *"I know that"*

the beautiful chaos of the yellow carnival and she stands
there.
there she is in her little black dress of solitude.
pretentious pretty girl, she waves at you,
with a little excitement, hiding the rest of it from me.
the way you look at her, the way she looks at you.

wish I didn't just realise you are not
by my side anymore.
with every footstep of yours
my heart cracks a little more.

but I choose to keep quiet. again.

there you are, thirty centimetres away from her.
and I see what?

that goddamn smile of yours
for which I fell harder than I should have.

I, now grip the pictures like you once gripped my waist.

//for I can still love you and let you go.//

~nayasha

I hope it's not.

will it be strange,
if I say I love you
but **I don't want
you to be mine?**

*(trust me, I tried,
yet, my lies stay untied,
tonight.)*

apologies for all
the **heaps of nonsense**
I wrote to you.
*(I meant each and
every word though)*

even if you don't
like me,
thanks for letting
me love you.

every time I try
drying out my tears,
just seconds
later, my vision gets

blur again.
the tear-soaked
pages of my diary
more like **the hurricane
of love, agony and pain.**

I'm afraid to get
closer to you,
like all others who make
you smile,
shit- I'm jealous
of the sight.

I'm afraid
maybe because I know,
I know that I'm gonna
leave the city soon,
around the end of
the dead's night.

*(and if I get closer,
it would be hard for me
to leave, right?)*

so, will it be strange,
if I say I love you

but I don't want
you to be mine?

~nayasha

under the blanket

under the blanket
we stayed,
motionless.

I still remember
the freezing winter night.
my head on your chest,

the rhythm of your heartbeat
the rhythm with which
my world revolved.

I gazed at you
your peaceful face,
happily resting on the pillow,
I gifted you.

the sound of
the burning wood,
the golden fireplace
truly, my golden hour-

no, sorry, the golden minute-
or maybe even,
the golden second.

you gripped me tightly,
tucked me right

beside you
you smiled,
your eyes closed.
guess, it was a pleasant
dream.
expected you to
say my name.
the way you did,
before falling asleep.

yes, expected.

expectations,
not my thing.
the only thing
I hate I possess.

you whispered
that one name,
you once told
I shouldn't be insecure
about.

the one name,
that made me paranoid.
that one name,
you had hidden me from,
for months, for years

and I stayed

motionless

under the blanket.

~nayasha

a story I'll never write

hope you could see
how I struggle to put down
my thoughts on paper.

the number of unrealistic
fantasies I make,
it's too difficult to explain.

moreover, I'm not good
at giving explanations, you see.

maybe, if I could share this
with you, you'd get a hang of it.

the kind of stories we
find in books and movies.

like how I'd look at you
if you were beside me.

how I'd call you
if I had the right
or had the courage, at least.

how I'd sing for
you **in the middle of the night.**

how you'd smile at me

from the corner of your eyes.
how you'd smirk
at the silliest things
amidst your video games,

your face coloured in
the neon hues from the screen,
an abstract art, I'd wish to paint.

but fortunately,
I know the difference
between dreams and expectations.
that puts me in a better place,
doesn't it?

my pillows, now,
aren't stuck between my tears
and my midnight complaints.

it took me a while to learn how
to sense the happiness
of the girl, **you're in love with.**

but,

I've learnt to smile at my mirror
as if it's you holding me from behind.

I've learnt how to end
a story I'll never write.

~nayasha

oddity

how odd it can be
to get haunted by
someone who's not dead?
being ripped into pieces

(in a prettier than
the usual brutal manner,
I guess)

with the teeth, you
have on your heart.
the same bunch of gnashers
you narrate your stories through.

or **those bloodless**
holes, my skin viciously possesses
fitting those secret paper
darts of yours.

chased by a maniac
I run around in circles.
round and round
on the thorny graves
round and round
inside my head.

it's not odd, is it?
to get haunted by someone,

who seems far from
*being the monster
under your bed.*

~nayasha

obscurity, my death

you crept in like hovering
darkness ready to engulf the cosmos.
this time, not even sparing
the little stars.

yet, I embraced you, saw you
as the **vignettes in my pictures.**
you made me bold,
I thought.

but only if I knew,
you made me hollow,
floating in singularity.

I smiled beneath the
transparent sheet

*(ironically, erasing the existence
of transparency)*

half drown in the black ocean,
the dark waves your eyes behold.
everything was perfect,
even for a heartbeat.

*(sometimes pretending
is a virtue)*

well, perfection, my love,
is suffocating.

a heart takes a heartbeat to stop,
as well.

if my heart stops,
you might disappear,
wouldn't that be good?

put my pictures
upon the dry bloodstains on
your wall
a bunch of petunias might be
helpful in making my
cold smile presentable,
or some casual paintings
of yours.

carve a sculpture out of my flesh,
brandings of forgotten love on my chest

//you're Picasso,
my darling,
help me die an aesthetic death.//

~nayasha

ps: just letting you know

I'm not mean but
I hope you regret it.

could still have been
immortalising you in
every verse I write.

but I butcher you with
every word I pen, instead.

you could still have been
the raining petals of
cherry blossom in my backyard.
**the place where I used to
picture you with a broken radio.**

but you are the thick
layer of polar ice where
I've stuck my soul, instead.

even if I know, the expectations
could kill me live,
I still hope you-

(to come back? You were never even there)

I still hope you know
that you were my doom
and I was doomed at
love's service.
now, *I need a new male lead*

for my stories

for my fantasies

for my madness.

and I know, it'd be too,
just a *blurry reflection of you.*

*//PS: this was a PS of a forgotten love letter.
Just letting you know//*

~nayasha

platonic heartbreak

1 AM can be beautiful

1 AM can be brutal.

1 AM haunts me

as I hang in between
beauty and brutality.

(platonic heartbreak, maybe?)

so bold of you to
assume I moved over you.
I mean I assumed it too
but assumptions-
there is something about them
*so certain yet drowning
in uncertainty.*

I could not write anything,

she lied,
the phantom within me.
she pinched my heart every time

I said I was fine.

(fine is never a feeling, remember.)

it was never about "I can't"
it always has been, "I didn't".

cause anything I wrote,
I would draw a sketch of you
in a place you've never been before,
that I'd never erase.

what magical yet a monstrous feeling, isn't it?

so I buried my diary
"assuming" I might get over you
but guess what, **death and life
are just two faces of the same coin,
so are you and poetry.**

*(oh for sure,
platonic heartbreak, it is.)*

~nayasha

ink might no longer flow

for the first time.
I was alone
in my favourite place.
ocean of thousand
known faces
but no one felt familiar.
I hoped my blazer
to be a little bit oversized
so that I could get
inside it and disappear.
my shoes felt heavy
so did my bag.
I hoped someone
could talk to me
but again I didn't want to.
the tears, I didn't let them flow.
haven't, actually, let them flow
for a while.
now, I have a clogged brain
flooded mind
blurry vision
wretched heart,

blocking everyone out
but you,
I hate you.
when you walked out
of that gate
with your pretty pretty girl.
(I can never hate her, I swear)
I wish I could turn volatile.
(dancing tear vapours under the
winter sun)
I wish I could erase my memory,
(I can't erase you, can I?)
I wish I should never have
wished for you.

I can take no more,
the petals of my heart,
the withering winter rose.
crumbled paper
all over my bedroom floor
but if I forget you, darling
my ink might no longer flow.

~nayasha

toom canvas

I stared at my blank notes
unable to frame a line
locked ourselves in the
school washroom cabin
my best friend and I,
thought we could write something,
something we couldn't express
in front of everyone.

she rushed her fingers on
her mobile screen
with a speed, **a sort of victory
over time.**
while I stared at my blank notes
unable to frame a line.

she walked out saying,
she'd wait for me in our class
and I tried again to
make sense of my senseless
thoughts.
I couldn't.
as I desperately searched
for the sparkle in my eyes,
but guess what! I never had them.

**there were just my frozen
tears glistening from your**

blinding lights.

and I stared at my blank notes
unable to frame a line.

I walked out and saw you
walking down the alley
at the middle of the corridor
you nodded your head
at me,
and beneath your mask
I hoped you smiled.
as I stared at my blank notes

*//yet in my head, I wrote a
thousand lines.//*

~nayasha

hologram

ten months hence,
I found myself standing
on that same stair,
on which you stood once.
the third last from
the landing.
the late February air,
the almost spring taste,
somehow I saw me
in front of you
in front of me.

ten months hence,
I found myself standing
in our old place,
still dumped with
whispers of your
soccer talks,
the unhindered laughs,
the forgotten secrets
and all those meaningless
scribbles,
on those broken desks
and peeled off walls.

ten months hence,
and I realized how fast
time skips.

and I wonder
how different we
could have been.
not like you broke me
not like you left me
what were we?
I guess it's still a mystery.

tens months hence,
I let out a breath
I didn't realize I
was holding,
standing amidst the
holograms of us
and I hope to live in
nostalgia of our

*not so Shakespearean
kind of love story.*

~nayasha

fibs in thy drawer

I wonder why I fall
so easily
am I that dearest to death?
I wonder what I am waiting for-
for you to love me back?
or for you to leave me as they did?
I thought I got someone new
but look where he took me to?
one more turn of the same old love
merry-go-round
one more round of miserable heartbroken words
but on a different horse, this time.
I wonder if I will ever get sick of it
(never, being a regular visitor of gloomy spring fair)

am I that dearest to death, then?
or worse still, the enemy of love?
I wonder if you'd ever know
(you won't, I swear, not at least as a confession)

I hope this isn't love
I hope I could explain it to you
the way I did in those unsent love letters
to someone I've never met
and I hope, you find them in *your drawer*
someday.

~nayasha

I'm falling backwards and I have you to blame

You were that one push
to the dominoes of my life
and since then they haven't
stopped falling for you.

they haven't stopped
lying overlapped on
each other like my words
when I hear you sing.

I try to run away
and what feels like **miles**
are **just a few inches**
between your guitar frets.

//I am falling backwards
and I have you to blame.//

~nayasha

the forbidden verse

sometimes,
I wonder if I should
quit poesy
because
you are brutal
and I don't want
to believe that **poetry
can ever be brutal.**

*// you are the verse,
I shouldn't be writing.//*

~**nayasha**

sorrows and symphonies

deliberate sombre notes
beneath my fingers
between the keys
I switch,
(hopefully graceful enough)
an overwhelming sadness
vocalising harmonies
an excruciatingly painful
high pitched bridge
between your verse of love
and chorus of lies.
I play
my fingers flowing
like yours, entangled in my hair
an eternity before
and.
and I die a little,
happily though
musical they sound
my patience, sorrows
and maybe their symphonies.

~nayasha

verre goutte de pluie

Trying their way in, the rain droplets,
through the fuzzy window
from the sky, a colour palette
of all shades of black and grey
the tiny *shapeless circles* of water
stick onto the glass shining
from the backlights
of the honking cars ahead
like the golden polka dots
on the black shirt of yours,
a confusion, a pretty
configuration of wrong stars
in my lucid dreams
I connect the dots
all the times
an infinite journey on a lane finite
they take me back
to the hour I lay on the
rained grass watching
Cassiopeia on an August night.

~nayasha

ugly hypothesis

every time your eyes
look for her voice,
somehow end up finding
mine
tracing the fading
junction between lovers
and friends, you let me
pray to own the kingdom
of your hidden obsession.

*(but friends don't play
 such games?)*

*//and the tales they've made of us,
I wish to carve a palace out of them//*

~nayasha

constant *(you'll always be)*

for all the wrong reasons I've loved you
and for all the right reasons you've never looked at me
that way,
I hereby drain all
the blood out of my heart-

a camphor to forever light the fire of

a warmth, I'd never
be a receiver of, but I hope I still get the
ashes of my heart back.

~nayasha

stairwell

I wonder, sometimes, if I am
climbing down a *stairwell*.
with each step, stands-
every guy I've liked.

And every time
I have liked someone,
I thought I've lost my heart
and *it's still the same.*

the stair I am standing on,
it's too inclined for me to balance.

but somehow I still hold on
and I think it's love
    (maybe).
if it's not, then,
   oh boy,
to be honest,
I am afraid of what real
love would seem like.

how *deep* would I have to
climb down?

for all I can see

is *darkness* when I try

looking at the bottom of the well.

//-but you'd push me, anyway//

~nayasha

our masquerade

put an arm around me
if you can
on **a blurry idea of friendship.**
on the same concept believing
which, you talk to me
about how much you like her.
let my head rest on your shoulder-
on the very same abstract.

speak nothing. search for the
ninety-nine hidden possibilities of 'us'
beneath the *golden rocks* we
rest our feet on.
let every thought that makes
me falter in my dreams
consume me.

I figure they are deep,
deep enough to make you
float in singularity.
you'd never know for

my words give no justice to them.

you don't seem to care,
though.
the way that **one** chance of you
and her in those *huge rolling*

waves has gotten all your
attention.

you smile at them.

I smile at you.

you think about her.

I think about you.

about me. about us
in places we've never
been before.

but

*// everyone talks about the
depths of the ocean but
no one questions what the
rocks hide.//*

~nayasha

10 pm, I cried last night

remainings of the red lipstick
but with a **little less transparency.**

I remember how my red dress
flowed down the black
granite slab. a little party that
my friend had thrown.

pretty couples. pretty loners.

**some clutched their broken hearts
in their leather jackets**
while some sipped
"less than lovers" drinks
amidst awkward smiles.

my stomach flipped to the
beat of our favourite song
that played on a loop outside
and inside I sat
my knees up to my chest
rummaging through the lyrics.

I don't know what happened

(maybe.
just maybe, I missed you, terribly)

tears rolled against my
embarrassed laugh. sniffs
between shaky breaths
somehow whispered your name.

(god, no. not again.)

but this is it. this is how I
claim.

10 at night

**in a washroom of a
fucking restaurant**

*// begging for footnotes in the
story of my life that you framed.//*

~nayasha

he loves me? he loves me not?

the backyard being my
recently most loved place.
(grasses are patient listeners)
the smell of approaching fall
lost in the void your words left behind.
the scripts meant for red wine
spoken by the stagnant grape juice.
and float in the air
my carefree secrets.
the glass kept untouched
on the *not-that-flowery* stained tablecloth,
soaked without any regrets, it was,
in the blood of my love.
"he is ignoring me. but he might be busy, right?"
"god. this is complicated."
while waiting for a reply
got only a like on my text.
well, *at least, he did that!*

my frustrated fingers traced

the patterns of the blue-on-white

british porcelain pot.

as I brutally asked the **daisy petals**

"he loves me? he loves me not?"

~nayasha

I'll dance

(after *d.s*)

I hoped there were grasses
underneath our feet.
the overwhelming silent cry
that overflowed
when you held my waist
could have touched the sombre
leaves.

at least,
you could have
been a *reason* for *someone's good.*

to the *perfect* song,
our hands glided but
she ran through your mind.
I took a turn, my dress twirled
you pulled me closer
I rested my head on your right
shoulder

and *you laughed.*

goddamn it.

(thought I had
stopped writing about
you long ago.)

we retraced those same strides
for a couple of minutes until
"do you know some other steps?"
you asked. you didn't wait for an
answer, though. you went away.

I stared down at my heels
to the last december,
all the shattered pieces of
my heart shimmered under
the chandelier.

would paste all those pieces
on that same dress, I wore yesterday.

(a hot glue gun is all I have)

and even at 3 am, if you asked
burn the past in shame,
in agony, I'll laugh

//blame all the deceitful
daisy petals
but certainly, I'll dance.//

~nayasha

anotsohiddenconfession

I have your name written on every
corner of my diary.
you see, I am not even the main
character of my own story.
you are.

my longest nights dream of you
but they're far from being loved by you.
(please tell me, I'm wrong)

'dear phosphenes' I've addressed you
in every entry.
because they never stop giving hopes
to the blinds.

I write you letters and post them
in my drawer.
big relief, my drawers are illiterate.
the letters are my secret possession

but today, I write
you. whatever this is.

a confession? (no?)

might just hide this too
wrapping it in a lovely pain.
so, crash into me
just for once,

// I swear,
you'll never have to fall again.//

~nayasha

where do broken hearts go?

last

december

someone shattered my
heart.

but

early

february

you glued it together.
the arrow of *ten months*
half held your friendship, half held
my love.

the latter never mattered
to you but our friendship is what
you held high

**(oh my- assumptions
always kill me slowly).**

it took only a

night for you to break that arrow
into two halves.

my love got stuck
inside my heart muscles *(it hurts
and that's okay)*

but you.

you burnt
the part of friendship,

**the suffocating
fumes of the last ounces of belief in
a friend danced on a chilly night.**

this.

this *fucking* hurts but oh, look, it's

december.

again.

but
this time

no

february

guitar can fix me.

because

*// december and february have been
playing hide and seek with me and god-
I can't even remember how long I have
been hiding. //*

~nayasha

a christmas carol?

oversized sweater, hot coffee
starbucks wasn't all that terrible.

(minus the paid singers who
ruined my favourite song.)

you live between my soaked
pillow and greasy hair.

and maybe,
your name's the only one
on my wishlist this christmas.
just saying though.
in case, you thought I don't
think about you anymore.

brownie crumbs that kissed the
rim of the glass held all fragments
of your sins but my sweater didn't
have the smell of your memories.

(everything about us is
so volatile, I'd rather live without
those memories, okay?)

but I never want the right things
in life, haha.

drink your guilt and smell your lies,
drown in your apologies
and die in whatever the *fuck* it was (or is).

my sister kept asking
if anything was wrong with me.

how could I tell her- my ways
to feel my heart is everything
that's wrong with me.

but christmas wasn't half as bad
as I expected it to be,
since you didn't text-
you never text, you see.

you always text **back.**

//santa likes to torture. he
was just a tale and so are his
gifts.//

~nayasha

guess, I didn't cry enough

last night, I looked at
my washroom mirror.
beautiful.

I looked
surprisingly beautiful.
beautiful enough **to gain
sympathy.**

red eyes smudged mascara,
stained cheeks, dripping
lipstick. oh my god.

***your sorrow makes me look
so pretty.***

played your playlist on
the loop and cried some more.
wanted to be prettier, you know.
prettier than the other
girl in the life of the guy
I am going to love in the future.

(future? when's that?)

cried some more, while
removing those coffee mugs
and manga books from my
shopping cart. *(I was waiting
for your birthday, by the way)*

deleting all the screenshots
of our face time, I cried a little
more. I still looked less beautiful than
the girl you like. how much does
she cry?

jesus. I could never-

*how could you sympathise with
someone so much that you start
loving them?*

~nayasha

icarus falls

and a catalogue of all the ways
you could break my heart
sticks to the confession page
of my diary

(you were my deputed diary,
by the way).

a gorgeously cruel surgeon you were,
crimson cheeks, red roses,
clever scalpel and a bunch of chrysanthemums
you placed by my grave.

I'm going to hide them
on the day of my wake, though.

and I remember when
imprisoned on the island
of heartbroken past stories, we met.

under my chest, my
ocean of love for you and over
the head, our **burning ego**
making up for the bright sun.

it's a pretty day of
unhindered chats. you clipped
wings of hope to my back

attached with **wax of my patience**.

but I soared too high
in the **mistaken sky**. hefty ego,
blazing fire defeated patience
within fractions of seconds.

the wax dripped down my torso
as fear did through my eyes.

I had sensed my death way too soon
yet in love, I chose to fly.

*//drown in the ocean, I obviously did
but unlike Icarus, I happily died.//*

~nayasha

fool's gold

in the aisle of our school bus.
amidst the tired faces,
screams so lively, we stood
(I mean, somehow managed to).

there were minutes when
speed breakers pulled us closer
and times when we were pushed apart.

and with all the beautiful
ways nature framed us,
it seemed like we were dancing,
to some random song that
the *once-introverted* guy
played on his guitar
in the back seat that somewhat
put the talks of the crowd
in tune.

the stories of the senior
school picnic, memories that were
being created and rumours that
were beginning to open up their wings.

sweet song and but you weren't
listening to it. you were sad about how
you couldn't talk to her; **oh god,**

**I can't possibly talk about us
without talking about her, right?**

six in the evening and streetlights
that we passed by glowed brighter
as you looked at them.

every time you were busy
humming songs for her, I spent
counting the times you smiled
when I joined in.

every time, you looked down
giggling thinking about
her, I waited for moments when you
mentioned me in between her thoughts.

you see the first day I got to know
about you, was the last day
I could fall for you because there was hope,

but I fell so hard
'cause you create that hope every day,
you piss me off, you say sorry
and I give in.

every time you hit me
with your words,
**I cover up the bruise with the
pieces of jewellery that you gift me
with every apology.**

"pure gold" your lips prompted.
I always have been bad
at comprehension, by the way.

fool's gold.
I close my eyes.

~nayasha

clouds don't bleed?

"you can't ask for something
from someone who doesn't have it,"
my mother smiles, and my tears
don't wait for hers.

love and promises we share,
but the tag of 'giving in' sticks to only
one's shoulders.

and compromise?

haha.

compromise never ends.
it builds up to become one's
dignity. a colossal mountain
behind and when it falls
on a fine morning, it hurts like hell,
and, the earth. it shudders every day.

droplets of disrespect condense
into huge clouds of blood and apologies.
**my mother fell for the wrong person-
and?**
    and,
    so did I.

~nayasha

if this is love, then love is dead

if you say, I can hide the
batteries of the clock
beneath the silk quilt of
memories that the winter despises.

thought I'd help you freeze time for *'us'*
remember? you said you'd stop the time
when I had stopped fighting with the digits.

all the time, time runs away
and now there's none to stop.

what if the clock on my wall
doesn't work-

the gifted watch drowned in her
scent spares no second

to make sure that you're miles
ahead of me but I don't mind.

I don't mind at all.

at least, I don't keep my
promises in a glass jar,
drop it **(obviously, by chance),**

and expect someone else to
step on the broken pieces
taking all the blame.

'love heals', they say.

~nayasha

honey ribs

people wait. but I can't.
I can't. I don't wait for you
to love me back. I complete
our story. with twists of my own and
no objections from you, obviously.
in a book that I hide beneath my mattress.
where *you* try to kiss the pendant between
my breasts that you gifted me
on the twentieth page. and I. I push you
back. **where I make patterns on the sand**
with my big toe all the while *you* stare at me
on the entire sixty-third page.
where on the ninety-eighth page
your honey-dipped fingers
trace each of my ribs until they set me
on fire. where on the hundred-and-fiftieth page
and more, **you can't help but**
hold my hands. where in the entire book
it's only you
tightening the knots that you've
been trying to loosen in reality.

and now, outside the bundled pages, I feel
naked. ants circle 'round
my rib cage, pinching off every
last ounce of honey of your touch
and with the loss of every gram,

I fall. I fall in love a little more with
your ignorance, innocence and you.

and the bitter part is, that I am afraid
I'll keep loving you without you
for a longer time than I loved you
when I had first tasted your presence.

~nayasha

I'll say I don't love you, anymore.

how could I even describe falling anymore?
I have been writing so much about
falling lately that absolutely nothing around
me seems to be rising. **(mind you. it has been
nothing but a dark night for Great Britain
for a year now.)**
all the delicate and beautiful things fall, you see;
raindrops, tears, snow, leaf and I. well, I fell
the hardest. so much so that the concrete
floor is cracked like the edges of my heart.
I remember you standing on it as if you'd catch me
even if I stumble. *(faulty observational skills alert.)*
but you walk over my ruptured blood vessels
every now and then. and I lay in the pool of
my blood sinking this ignorant heart of mine
as I see you leave with my canoe and roses
that you plucked from my garden.

*// after all, we are just seeds in someone else's
land. //*

~nayasha

a lost apostle

apologize.

apparently, that's what
I have been
doing since the beginning.

I fall, I am sorry.
you fall, I am sorry.

slip my fingers on my screen
and press that arrow of sent.

(the arrow through my heart
that held me together,
a piece of it went away with you.)

who am I supposed to
apologise to?

to you, for pushing you away
or
to me, for letting you go?

(I swear I have never been
this anxious to make sense out of my words.)

"hope" and *"expect"* are the words
that hurt me more than my bruised skin.
they wash away all the truth
filling my heart with a made-up reality.

you.

you were probably
my made-up reality.

I *expected* you'd ask
you, I *hoped, expected* I'd explain.
I wish I could tell you to come back,
but my ego knocks my knuckles
every time I make up my mind to text you.

(I half believe it's your fault)
our friendship lost against my ego
       (your ego)

we lost us.
I lost you.

~nayasha

kaleidoscope

I had been looking into
the kaleidoscope from the
wrong side all this while
and wondered
why the moonlight never sparkled
the rivers that flood my eyes.

~nayasha

my mom loves you

I have exhausted
all my ideas forming
new stories about you every
day to tell my mom so that
she never asks
*"What about the boy you
used to talk about often?"*

What about him, mom?

he never wanted to be the
love interest in my story
because it'd have been too perfect.

and your daughter, could
never be that-

perfect.

~nayasha

pretentious little boy

I've never been in love.
been in always betrayals rather.
I've always been living in the room
whose windows you've been
breaking with your soccer ball.
but the shattered pieces of glass
show me how delicate I look.

desperate.

desperately waiting for you
to come and ask if I am okay.
but you don't until the one day
when there isn't a single piece of glass
dangling down from my window frames
and the soccer ball hits my head.
that's when you ask if I am okay-

-asking a dead if she's able to breathe.

~nayasha

to my ocean of calmness

I'd never ask you about the reasons
behind you turning so reckless lately.
(unlike one of my friends. god, she's
so upset about that day that she spent
without her man).

I'd never question your uncertainty
the cyclonic tensions that you've been
creating, because I know.

I know, no matter how calm you may
seem to others, at the end of the day, you'd
drown me. **you'd drown me so bad.**

but I'd still love you from the darkest
corners of your life. I don't mind
wherever you keep me. I'll still love you.

// I'll love you till "forever" is scared. //

~nayasha

he is poetry between my words, stories under my tongue
and pretty eventful deaths in my life.
he is everything, I didn't want him to be.

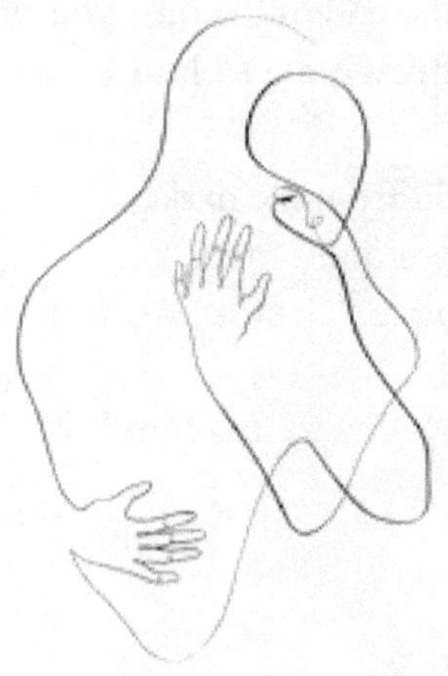

1

There's a station and you're there to go back to your hometown. You have no idea whether you've already missed the train or you're quite early. There's no one on the platform. Just you and the silence of the rest of the world. Your thoughts are revolting in themselves. You wonder if there'd be enough space for you on the train. What if it's crowded? What if you get hurt while you try to get on it? You hear a faint train whistle but you're not sure if the noise is fading in or fading out. There's a commotion somewhere hidden underneath the superficial peace you've been standing in. But you've got no choice but to wait. And *'how long'* isn't something you can answer.

I hate this. I hate how much I love *him*. I hate how *his* voice shatters me and builds me up at the same time. I hate that *his* voice makes me feel like I am drunk yet at the same time, it's my sober. *His* eyes, so deep, like waves of black ocean. Dangerous to dive in but I am still tempted to jump into it, explore and feel the waves of love.

It's sickening to realise that my love for *him* confuses me more than it makes me happy.

⁜

2

So, this is how falling in love feels like? Frightening yet peaceful at the same time. The feeling of getting hung between the poles of uncertainties and tied with the wire of a certain deep affectionate feeling.

The more I talk to *him*, the more deeply I fall for *him*. I am so used to silently loving *him* that *his talking about the girl he likes feels like an ant bite, but it still hurts*. It hurts that *he* shares everything with me but then that's something I crave for. *He* is like an open theme, everything that's under the Sun. And it takes me minutes, hours and sometimes, days to form sentences that would describe *him*.

A guy with a guitar whom I first got to know about through a virtual screen. A bandage to my winter wound, the last December when another guy had broken my heart. Not really broken, now that I realise. *He* just cracked it a bit but *he* got inside, tangled within the strings and mend it and *he* breaks it so calmly from within it every time I want *him* to hold the strings more firmly.

God, what is this power that you've given him?

$$\vdots\!\!+\!\!\vdots$$

3

I'm so afraid to lose *him* and I'd never know *his* point of view. And it disappoints me even more. Makes me anxious every time, I think about it. If there was a chance to ask for a superpower, I'd definitely ask for mind infiltration (as I've already said before). *Does **he** even think about me when I'm not talking to **him**?*

I try so hard not to make *him* mad. I'd start my every sentence with an apology if that means *he'd* stay in my life. That is so self-infuriating if you think, but I can't help it. No matter, how many guys I like, *he* is the one who feels like home to me. A soothing sensation. An unsaid belief that *he* saves all my secrets more safely than I do. Maybe, *he* does or maybe *he* just lets them go into the nothingness of *his* utter carelessness.

He is always on my mind, back of it if not the main one at the moment. In everything I write, I try to squeeze *him* between the lines. *He* is such an effortless and efficient thief of my time. I envy *him*. *He* is so fluid with whatever *he* does to me. Talk, share, make me fall harder and then talk again but this time about the girl *he* likes. No, *he* is not obliged to love me back but from all the guys I've ever liked, *he* seems to be the hardest one to move over. Probably because *he* is one of my best friends.

So, I am pretending that I am over *him* and I believe that one day, I don't have to pretend anymore. But ***'after him'*** might be my ***'afterlife'***.

❖ ❖ ❖

4

We never look directly towards the sun, do we? We prefer to look at the shadows created by its light, instead. The shadow of fire on my walls looks like a flower but I never noticed that it kept eating up the wood pieces that gave it a place to live. We never look at things directly, we look at what we are made to see.

We never realise how loving a person could destroy us because it's all grey in there. No lines of the boundary. No imperfections. Even the scars of a fallen angel seem to be hidden in her shadows. We think it's a wildflower when it's just a monstrous tale of fire. That's what makes people say *'love's blind'*.

But being blind is not *'not being able to see'* but rather it's when you *'don't perceive what you see'*.

⌘

5

I spent the entire month pretending I don't love *him* and god, I am never doing that. I felt like throttling myself. I felt the punch every time *he* took her name while we talked. When she rejected *him*, I wanted to be sad because *he* is my friend but somewhere inside, I was happy because I am the girl who is in love with *him*.

It is not complicated as I am making it but only if I wasn't a deluded soul. The worst combination of a person would be a deluded, depressed teenage love poet going on a one-sided love ride. There are people lucky enough to get the love that they want but *love* loves to get caught in careless hands and escape needful hearts.

Love's always afraid of my heart and my heart, well, it cannot afford to convince love. My heart cannot afford to convince *him*. I've been writing the entire day because

I want to write about *him* and that's how I tell *him* that I love *him*. Only if- only if *he* could read these.

Well, if you're reading this, someday, somewhere, I wish you could just text me that you love me too. I wish you could tell me it's not just me hanging from a single rope from the cliff and that you're clinging to it as well from the other side. One day, I hope we both climb it up, together, making all my poems and all my entries meaningless.

Just one day, I hope.

6

I hope we were together and then you would have broken my heart. I could have blamed you for everything. But in this one-way love, it's all on me. And I'm not that good at taking all the blames. It's burdening my chest along with all the untold love I have inside it.

If it gets all mixed up, I'm afraid it'll turn into this huge hurricane I won't be having control of. And I can't even blame you for the consequences. Like the first shower drop in the winter mornings, it would feel and the painful events will grow into *'you not talking to me anymore'*.

With all the blame games I am playing with myself, I somehow realise that I won't be able to get out of this huge mess. Circles made up of the strings of your new guitar that you bought with my choice have trapped me so tight, I doubt I could ever let anyone untangle them.

You promised you would never leave me. You said you weren't like others. You swore on my poetry that we would always watch the stars fall, together. You assured me that I wouldn't be hurt in the tent of your friendship. You told me, you understood me. You promised that you would never let the fire inside me die.

Then why do I find myself lonely and misunderstood and shivering under a torn tent, facing a dying fire, under a starless night? Why do I write a line less than the previous day, every day?

Why is it that everything I write about you is in the past tense?

⌗

7

What if I invite you to one of my parties and then you fall in love with me?

What if you hold me from behind while I make my signature trippy lotus flower drink for you?

What if I co-incidentally wear a dress of your favourite colour?

What if you love the shade of my lipstick so much that you'd like to taste it?

What if we make love and become one and never part ways?

What if you fall harder for me than I had for you?

The answers to these questions are never my concern,
though. The questions in themselves are so satisfying
that I don't have to wait for their answers. I could set an
entire scene in my head and the next moment, I'd wake
up to reality because of my 6 am alarm, check texts from
you talking about how your date with her went last night.

All those *'what ifs'* vanish within a few texts and a few
minutes. It's so heart-wrenching, sometimes. I wish I had
left you unread.

The first time you texted me and every time you text me.

＃

8

This time, I pressed *send*. Mad respect for my guts, though. And maybe, a few credits to my Spotify playlist that made me frustrated enough to not worry about the consequences of hitting that *send*. I mean I half expected you to say that you've realized how much I love you but instead, you said that you understand my situation and asked me to take my time figuring out my feelings.

What else do I need to figure out?

I have taken enough time to realize that I was wrong about getting over you just the way I did before. People say that you might not be the love of my life. Oh my god, how deep does real love go? *Oh! what's deeper than this lovely heart crack?*

I am seeing you in everyone and you're slowly becoming an illusion. It's so sickening when I try to think about you not being with me. What did I see in you? Probably, everything I needed at that time and slowly, you became a habit. *A bad habit.* Now, I pass hours counting seconds in between your messages.

I don't know where this is heading but wherever I'll stand, your voice would be the rustle of the leaves of the trees, your breath would be the ultimate wound-healing breeze, your words would be the speed breaker of my pulse rate, mind you. *And of course, wherever I'd stand, I'd colour the sky with my love for you.*

✦ ✦ ✦

⌗

9

It's so hard to believe in your words, sometimes. It's like I am putting my heart into a showcase of a stall in a seasonal fair, all open for everyone to see what a masterpiece you've created out of this lifeless mass of muscles and flesh. Stitches and cracks everywhere and dripping blood from a side.
An authentic design, isn't it? What do they call it?

Aesthetic.

I hope it's *aesthetic* enough for their eyes. A vintage portrait of your favourite crime *(I hope)*. But I am blind *(I'll just deliberately close my eyes)*. I love how my heart looks. All painful and sorrowful enough to grab your **sympathy.**

Your love's too costly. I don't know what *she* did to earn
it. I want to talk to her. I want to know what's in her that
still glues you to her even after how gracefully she
stumped upon your heart *(but she could never be as
great as you are at this)*.

I mean white bandages look better than heel prints, at
least on the muscular surfaces, I guess. It depends,
though. You might like less beautiful things and I might
like things that are actually pretty *(and dangerous)*.

Seasonal fair in the middle of nowhere, and all stalls are
empty but yours. A crowd of *pathetic people* form a
haphazard pattern in front of it and you hold *my heart*
high.

10

Is my cry for help too faint?

A mere attachment can flip your life upside down.
Noted?

I've never fiddled with my fingers while writing
anything. I'm doing nothing but trying to make sense out
of my thoughts. My head is heavy and muddled. The
fear of never getting loved the way I wished for, haunts
me morbidly.

My life has become a language I no longer understand.
The beauty of the shapes and patterns of the letters is all
I live for *(which rarely shows up only when I talk to*

him). I feel ashamed writing all of these. A self-loving person would want to burn my book. Go ahead, I won't stop. But I can never bring my heart to love myself the way I see some people do. I like to be truthful, you see.

And the truth is, I am never enough.

11

There could be countless numbers of letters rotting
inside my drawer. A common address is attached to all
of them. There's no point in posting them since he is not
into literature *(yet I've made him my favourite
character)*.

He'd never get the emotion lying underneath my words.
He'd never get the references hidden between the
syllables, waiting for him to find them. But once, he sent
me a diary entry of the day he got rejected by the girl he
likes and oh my god, heartbreaks can turn anyone into a
writer.

I was happy because *he* wasn't sad *because* of me but
cried inside because *he* wasn't sad *for* me. The way *he*
ended *his* entry with the nickname she gave to *him*. But

he never gave me a nickname and I never put a question.
He rarely called me by my name.

His text would always start abruptly *(exactly the way he entered into my life)* and the conversation mostly ends without a proper 'bye' *(obviously, not the way I want him to exit my life)*.

On second thought, proper 'goodbyes' are hard because the last hope *crumbles*.

12

I'm sure if I slit my wrists, I'd find the red wine I had been drinking all this time while loving you instead of my blood. My lipstick stain on the glass that says all those stories you always ask me to share with you glitters under my radiant pain. I've kept it safe on my shelf and I hope you still have the broken bottle you stabbed me with.

⌘

13

He is a beautiful poem in my life.

Rest, it's upon *him* if *he* wants to be
the *'beautifully happy'* kind or the *'beautifully sad'*.

or maybe, *'the beautifully complicated'* kind.

◆ ◆ ◆

14

No matter how many corners I visit inside my brain, it's his memories that I find playing in my inbuilt camcorder. Oh god, I just hope I am not in love with him.

I hope I am in love with the versions I created of him.

✦ ✦ ✦

＃

15

Recently, I felt a flip in my stomach when I met a boy
who looked so much like *him.*

It makes me frown when I think how much control *he*
has over me even when *he* is not even with me. There's
so much about *him* that can be felt. I have been writing
for two years now but still can't put my thoughts into
words, *he* is THAT messed up inside my mind.

People say literature is magic. Sure, it is. But *he* is
something beyond magic, beyond illusion, beyond
poetry, beyond stories and *beyond literature.*

✦ ✦ ✦

16

Sometimes, I wonder what if he has a best friend *(who's obviously not me. I never was, to begin with.)* to whom he talks about his everyday life and all the things that happen to him. What if their conversation starts with him complaining about how annoying I am? Imagine being all sweet to you and then one just goes and badmouths you in front of another. How pathetic is that? I must trust him but I don't. I can't anymore since that day.
The day when I got to know that friendship dwells upon sympathy as well. But it's weak, of course. Sympathy is like a substitute for love. A low-cost replacement. But it doesn't keep things fixed forever. Someday, it has to cause pain inside of us. And it's so sad that pain makes us okay with situations we aren't even okay with. That pain is sometimes, mistaken for love.
And that's how most of us live. *Ignorant.*

◆ ◆ ◆

⊞

17

Falling for *you* wasn't falling at all if I think. It felt like I was walking through a long dark hallway and suddenly, found an unexpected door. I opened it and it was all so bright. Blinding. It was then that I realised that *I was home*.

But homes are dark as well, for the blinds, aren't they?

I loved *you* in prayers and *you* left me in
the pool of curses that I created.

◆ ◆ ◆

18

I would be sitting with an ink-filled pen and an empty mind the entire day. *But you're on my mind.* Does that mean **you're nothing**?

Hopefully, you're just an idea I thought of because I was too afraid to fall in love with a real person.

Hopefully, my hopes are just mere hopes.

19

Why did God give ridges on my palms if they weren't
meant to hold *his* name?

⠿

20

Every ounce of my patience has been used to nourish the
fire that is lit between us. The one that burnt our
friendship. The fire that *you* had lit and I did nothing to
extinguish it. I did nothing and instead, I let myself burn
in it. Someone else replying to your one-page long
'sorry' paragraph on my behalf, says it all, cause I've
said enough.

*You've stolen all my words and there's nothing left in my
dictionary. Just spotless white pages and my tear stains
on them.*

✦ ✦ ✦

⊞

21

Six in the morning and I'm still here.

(Half busy waiting for your texts and half busy making
excuses for being late to school today.)

How do I tell that you've broken double the things
you've mended in my life?

How do I say that I still have nothing but love for you?

(I know my best friend's going to kill me for this.)

Every morning, I try writing a line that would tear through people's hearts. But somehow, I can't.

Guess, love has hit people harder than any poetry could ever do.

22

If only you had said *"it'll pass"* when I said, *"I love you"*.

♦ ♦ ♦

23

You would say, **"Nayasha, I gave you my hand for friendship but I never said to wrap it around your neck."** I did wrap it, I agree but *throttling me* was your choice and *mistaking pain for love* was mine.

◆ ◆ ◆

24

I would never say that you lighted up my world like nobody else did but you were certainly the one I believed who'd *never let my world turn into a dark palace.*

But beliefs are just thoughts and those thoughts exist in my mind and everything that's in my mind can't be real. Some seem perfect being fictional, darling. And no, I'm definitely not **talking about you.**

25

I talked of *"**forever**"* and *he* spoke of *"**nows**"*.

◆ ◆ ◆

26

From the day I have known *him*, I have become a visitor to my own mind. *His* thoughts could take my life. They take my life. Every time. I am a living dead and those thoughts, *Jesus*. They are so revolting. *He* doesn't even care, does *he*?

Maybe, I am just the annoying contact in *his* chat list that *he* replies to because *he* clicks on it by mistake. *(But every time?)*

I was healing, to be honest.

And then he comes up with *his* "sorry" as if that's going to fix my ruptured blood vessels. *But it works. Right, Nayasha?* I am starting to feel bad for myself which I should have way before, by the way. Why do I give in so easily?

I'd never know if I ever start to sell my peace of mind, in huge mugs that were meant for whiskeys *at the bar that **he** inherited from one of **his** distant uncles.*

27

Hope. It's terrifying that I could still think of "hope".
How could I even-

Tongue-tied, truly. I am not even trying to justify my
actions, anymore. (Great job?). Guess, I had been hiding
more than I could even realise. I didn't know the
different sides that exist to me.

I wonder if that makes me the moon.

I wonder if that'd make you fall in love with me.

There's so much love inside me that could literally
suffocate you to *death*. Maybe, you know that and
perhaps, that's why. That's why you never try to open up

that side of me because you know it's dark. Because you know that's the lunar eclipse- the shadow of my love, angst and disappointment. And you're scared.

Fuck. You're scared.

⌖

28

At what point in time, am I finally going to stop writing about you? Complicated answer, han?

Maybe, as the book ends?

Maybe, now?

Maybe, *never?*

For all the things you've done to me, good or bad. This is the payback. For every time, you wanted to live, I immortalised you and for every time you wanted to *die,* honey, *I immortalised you.*

✦ ✦ ✦

⁜

29

My grandma has a little garden on her terrace. It looks so beautiful in the morning, in the afternoon, evening and at night and every time. It's peaceful. I once heard the flowers complain about how they've been doubting that it's your thought and not their beauty that makes me smile. I felt bad. I said sorry. I said it was not true. *You can't possibly manipulate yourself, right?* But sweety, they were actually, seriously, literally jealous of you. But we bonded over *'how we can't get what we want'* daily chats. Those million little petals told me stories about their untold love for the little bumblebees who *just* wanted to be *friends* but-

You know what.

◆ ◆ ◆

30

"There was before you and there was during you. For some reason, I never thought there would be an after you."

~Colleen Hoover (Reminders of Him)

When I read the book three months ago, it was overwhelmingly sad. Now that each word is starting to sink into my skin, I can't even cry. There are no tears left inside me. I am a dried pen.

Fifteen minutes were all it took for *him* to put a full stop to a friendship of *ten* months. On a scale of 1-10, how silly does that sound? I had lost my love long ago and now, I have lost one of my closest friends. *(I feel like an orphan.)*

Thought, I was writing about unrequited love all this while but never knew the roof that sheltered me was built up with bricks of *unrequited friendship.* Is that even a term? Maybe. I created it. **He** *created it.* How genius.

I had so much to write but unfortunately, I can't write on wet pages. The ink spreads like shapeless mandala art. *(lost love and floating friendship can make beautiful patterns 'at the very least', okay?)* Today, I star-marked all your texts, so that later I would have something to hurt myself with. *Effortlessly suicidal,* you see. Of course, nothing's more painful than your sweet *sympathetic* messages.

Just two days ago, I wished to cross paths with your bright smile in a random crowded street and today, I'm afraid of romantic accidents. Just how love turns phases.

What is love if not wanting you from every one of the million pieces that you broke my heart into?

31

So much to take in and no way to let them out. I feel
saturated. I can't even bring myself to delete *his* playlist.
7 in the morning and I am crying even to the happy
songs in it. Too much shredding of tears, isn't it?

Isn't that something I've been doing since the start of the
book? What is crying actually? Letting out an
overflowing emotion, right? That's all this entire book is
about. Letting out my love for *him* in some way or the
other through my poems and notes.

If only I was given a chance to love *him* in real life. If
only *he* ever chanced upon my diary and I swear, *he*
would have fallen in love with *himself*. There's so much

love hidden beneath the silence of my words, hidden beneath the patience I held until *he* texted me back, hidden beneath the calls I received from *him* even when I was half asleep. I gave so much and got nothing in return. Actually, I never wanted anything but only the allowance of *loving him forever.*

But where the hell did I go wrong? Did putting myself over my love cost me his absence in my life?

Oh, well, I'm so sorry, I fell.

32

Imagine getting comments under your each and every Instagram post from that one particular person and then suddenly, one day, you don't get them anymore. The excitement of the new post goes away, right?

A person, some ten-fifteen years elder than me reading my book might think how shallow love has become. It hasn't. Trust me. Just the ways of expressing one's love have changed. 90s kids would want to write letters but a teen of today would obviously want a reply to their story particularly posted for that one person. *Letters are still chef kisses, BY THE WAY.*

Why am I saying this to you? Well, because I am not getting *his* comments on my posts anymore. It's sad. It's really sad. I, somehow, am still holding on to my intuition that *he* would come back. *He'd* say that *he* has realised that *he* needs me. Everyone wants to be needed, isn't it? But *his* last words still haunt me. I knew *he* was always bad at literature but that doesn't mean he'd use words that he didn't even mean. *(Assumptions.)* He labelled our *(my)* friendship as a mere *sympathetic* companionship-

No matter if *he* blames *himself* for whichever kind of strangers we are now but I'm sorry, I don't think I was that bad of a friend.

But he wasn't either.

✦ ✦ ✦

33

I was just watching a tv series. A very interesting crime thriller, indeed. There came a scene where the girl talks about how the guy ghosted her after giving her hope during the entire summer. Sounds pretty much like *you*, isn't it?

And I paused it.

Partly, because there was a weird feeling boiling inside my stomach and mostly because the screen wasn't visible to me properly. *It was starting to get blurry.*

I wasn't crying. I didn't scrunch up my nose or made a weird expression. Neither did I look sad, to be honest. The tears just *flowed.*

It's like the void that you left behind in me was
constantly getting filled with my tears and imagining my
body as a bottle, the tears were already up to the neck of
it. Her lines were the last few drops that made it
overflow.

I don't know how many times I've read your last texts. I
have lost count, not going to lie. I guess I have said
about it before.

God, there's so much to say about you that I forget what
I have already said and what else is left to say. I am
going through all my notes once again because repeating
the same old gossip would be annoying for my readers,
right?

Little things are starting to trigger me so much
since you've been gone.

34

One of my friends once said, *"Almost is the saddest word in the English dictionary"*.

I couldn't get what she really meant back then until you *almost* became a part of me. When you *almost* made me believe that I could be loved the way I want to be. When we *almost* made it. But it never happened. The word 'almost' gives unrealistic hopes which at a point *almost* seem to get real. When I *almost* put a heart next to your contact name. But you shrugged it off and now-

now, your name has a broken heart beside it, a secret possession of mine kept safely in the archived list of my chat.

◆ ◆ ◆

35

Dot twelve and I wonder why I am not asleep yet. Well, probably because I am determined to write something today. It's always the same, writing about you. It starts with vigorous biting of nails and trying to think of pretty-enough lines to leave people breathless. It's never easy writing about you *(I think I have said this before, god)*. Movies give you all kinds of bullshit. Falling is not easy at all. Never effortless, trust me. Excuse me if I end up contradicting any of my other notes because my notes are never well-thought orderly arranged words. I just write what I think and I swear, these notes will drive people crazy. These will make people rethink my mental condition. *(I am okay. I just think a lot and ironically, I don't know how to put them in a sequence that'd make sense.)* These notes will confuse them because I don't know what I want. And that's the whole point of writing them down, to check how insane he has driven me. To

check if I am good enough to survive the rest of my life.
To check if I am understood-

*because there's no one more misunderstood than a poet
stuck between "dear love" and "yours lovingly" in a
forgotten love letter to that someone who doesn't even
know that they've been the favourite in an ocean of many
books.*

♦ ♦ ♦

＃

36

You'd list all your felonies in the pretty notebook of
yours that you played FLAMES in and nothing would
even come close to the pit that you've left half-dug
inside my chest when you let me go.

Should have safely handled my heart or should have
crumbled it into micro-fragments but all you did was put
in a crack. A permanent, unsealable, deep crack.

My trust now stands like the ace of red hearts kept at the
top of the house of cards-

*(our house. Our house where you've promised to not
repeat the same mistake again for what? A forty-third
time, maybe?)*

Your ignorance is that table fan my father always used to
keep switched on near my study table and guess what-
**I never had a house made up of cards in my life
before.**

⠿

37

Why doesn't love come with a disclaimer?

But on second thoughts, that wouldn't make sense, right?
Because in love, every time, everyone, everything gets
harmed in some way or the other.

People get reminded of beautiful things when they think
about their loved ones.

Not in my case. No. You don't remind me of pretty
mountains or butterflies or roses or anything. In fact, you
remind me of nothing. I forget about everything else
when I think about you. Your thoughts are so blinding, I
wonder why the winged cupid is painted blind. I try to
lose every memory of yours hoping that the entire jigsaw

puzzle of the lover girl inside of me disassociates. Unfortunately, those memories turned out to be those disastrous clothes of mine that I deliberately tuck into the back of the almirah just to see my mother forcing me to wear them the very next day. Irresistible, frustrating, yet I feel attached to them. The clothes. The memories.

Because trying to forget someone you love is like remembering someone you've never met.

38

"Could you please be consistent at doing at least one thing?"

I don't remember how many times Mamma would have said this statement over the last sixteen years. And now I hesitate to bring myself up to think about how I could love you for this long. How could I stick to loving that one guy who doesn't even care about me? If only I could inform her about this achievement. I am sure she'd be happy about my consistency minus the 'being in love' part.

We all understand Mamma, don't we?

But that's not the thing.

*The thing is, the way to your heart is a one-way lane and
I am that one unlucky car that has been stuck in the
slowest-moving row.*

But eventually, I'll reach my destination, right?

⌗

39

My heart. Holy shit. What a rebellious bitch! I remember
my best friend saying *"How do you fall for every guy so
quickly? And then after a few months, he's gone and you
fall for a new one. That's not how it happens."*

That's not how it happens?

And every time, I felt I was getting over you, I forced
myself to keep loving you. Why? Because
oh,
that's **exactly how it happens**.

❖ ❖ ❖

40

He feels hurt because *he* was never taken care of by the girl *he* liked and I feel the pain because *he* cared too much, and then left suddenly. *He* wishes she cared a little more and I wish *he* never cared at all. The thing between us was never solid, you see. It was all made up of feathers of wishes and hopes and dreams and-
and lies?

Maybe. That's why I wonder why the feathers never danced away with the brutal breezes. The bones of lies held them all together.

The bones, mostly mine…the lies, mostly his.

✦ ✦ ✦

⌗

41

Last note. Fewer stories to share or more like no stories to share at all. I feel like I have written enough not to sink into my couch for the next couple of months, I guess. But not enough to be able to burn the polaroid of *him* and I that I had clicked inside of my head with the camera that my cousin gifted to me.

The poses that I have imagined are so vague but they constantly keep flashing in while I am asleep. *I'm in love with him while I'm asleep.* They keep fading in while I am walking down to my neighbourhood park. *I'm in love with him while I'm walking.* They keep putting themselves up in the hidden museum of my lovely fantasies.

I'm in love with him while everything I do. I am in love with him while I'm alive. I'd be in love with him even in my afterlife. But *he* must let me go. We don't have what it takes and *he* doesn't even like me *(that way? In none ways, darling, in none ways.)*

Love is like a rubber band, holding two persons together. It's sad that people only relate love to romantic ideas I am not only talking about the romantic ones, be it motherly, fatherly, brotherly or platonic love. When one person leaves, it hurts the other.

Writing this book is a way of letting him go but I'm so used to being with *him*. It is so peaceful *talking to him* but so painful *talking about him*. I tried the *'21 days'* of not speaking to *him* which one of my friends suggested would help.

Didn't work.

The notification of his texts somehow pops up between my heart and my brain and I lose the battle. The war was always within me and I lose it every time his name shows up on my screen. The funny part is, I don't even repair the cracked screen of my phone because I like to see his name that way. Broken. No matter how sadistic that sounds but that's the only way I could break him. *(I don't want to hurt him in real life, though.)*

He makes me break my own rules. I can't live until *he* is alive, but as I said already, I can't possibly kill *him*, right? Not even in my head. *Guess, it's me dying either way.*

The fact that hurts the most is he is (still) my best friend
(for me. I don't care about his pov. or maybe, a little bit.)
He was my *'dear diary'*, but I didn't realise that- *diaries
too have a last page.*

♦ ♦ ♦

i

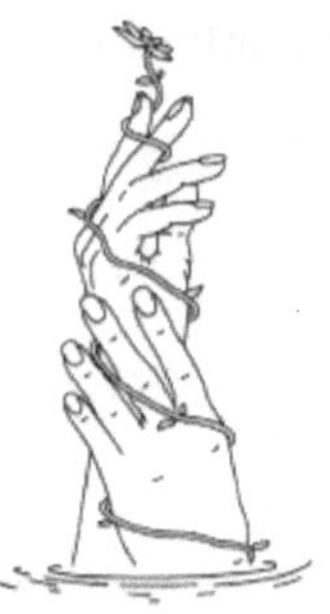

fell.

for all those who think this was
a work of fiction,

it was.

"The hell?
This book has two dedication pages?!"
Yes. And?

You've made it to the end of this delicate map
of my soul *(not exactly)* which led you to
nowhere. Thank You. You guys are the best.

<3

about the author

Nayasha Jena is an awkward girl. That's because she knows that the most absurd things fly out of her mouth whenever she starts to talk. So she writes. That way, she can strike out parts that don't make sense. When the 17-year-old poet isn't busy filling pages in her diary, she is undoubtedly messing up with her mother's belongings, stealing pens from her father's drawer, eating cake pops and trying to decipher the meaning of life while blankly staring at her academic books. A self-taught artist, she can also be found smiling amidst crumpled papers, lead fingerprints and eraser dust. As obsessed as she is with music, she absolutely loves the idea of her concert which, unfortunately, ends within her bedroom walls. She read her first novel in eighth grade and has been addicted to literature ever since. From romance to crime thrillers, she treasures novels of every genre. Nayasha claims that literature is the way of life. Every action could be forged into a story and the unsaid feelings could be weaved into poetry. She believes that *literature is a textually transmitted disease.*